WELSH NARROW GAUGE RAILWAYS
FROM OLD PICTURE POSTCARDS

by

ANDREW NEALE

Plateway Press, P.O. Box 973, Brighton, BN2 2TG
ISBN 1 871980 08 9

ACKNOWLEDGEMENTS

I owe a special debt of gratitude to Brian Hilton, who has given me full access to his postcard collection, and permission to reproduce cards in this volume. Other sources of illustrations are: G. Alliez, Dave Brewer, Vic Bradley, Philip Hindley, the Industrial Railway Society, Frank Jones, Lens of Sutton, the Locomotive Club of Great Britain, Maid Marian Locomotive Fund, Jim Peden, Photomatic Ltd., the Talyllyn Railway Co., Simon Townsend, J. Valentine & Co., the Welsh Highland Light Railway Co., the Welshpool & Llanfair Railway Co., D. W. Winkworth; my thanks are due to all of them for their contributions.

John Harrison and Simon Townsend contributed information for the 'Fairbourne' and 'Rhyl' captions (though responsibility for any errors rests with Plateway Press). The map was drawn by David H. Smith. Finally although for the sake of simplicity this volume appears under my name, like all 'in-house' Plateway titles it is very much a joint effort between myself and Keith Taylorson, who has contributed information (particularly on the postcard history aspect) to the captions, supplied cards and photos from his collection, and was responsible for book design, layout and production.

ANDREW NEALE
Leeds, March 1991

Printed in Great Britain by Wayzgoose plc, East Road, Sleaford, Lincs.

ISBN 1 871980 08 9

Front cover illustration: Thanks to the Edwardian postcard publisher, views of long-lost railways are available in colour. The Glyn Valley Tramway's 0-4-2T SIR THEODORE poses with a Chirk bound train at Ponfadog around 1910, on a 'Gwenfro' series artist-coloured card.

Back cover illustration: An evocative view from the early days of railway preservation. Talyllyn Railway No. 4 EDWARD THOMAS is pictured at Abergynolwyn in the early 1950's, on a tinted card from Valentine's.

Frontispiece: In the heyday of Corris Railway passenger services, one of the Hughes 0-4-2T's is seen at Machynlleth with a train of handsome bogie coaches, rebuilt locally from older four-wheelers.

PREFACE

"History, like dry G.W.R. rail sand, has a habit of slipping through the fingers and is gone before you can save it. Old postcards help to stem the flow and prevent a total loss." So ran the most eloquent review* of our first book *Narrow Gauge and Miniature Railways from Old Picture Postcards* (Plateway Press, 1986). That book surveyed the entire field of narrow gauge and miniature railways in Great Britain - plus a representative selection from overseas - and inevitably within its 64 pages there was scope for only a token coverage of even the most significant of Britain's narrow gauge railways.

Nowhere was this more so than in the case of Wales, indisputably the birthplace of the modern narrow gauge railway, as the opening of the (horse-worked) 2ft gauge Penrhyn Quarry tramroad in 1801 proved the viability of the narrow gauge in transporting large quantities of traffic, and the successful introduction of steam traction on the Festiniog Railway in 1863 - confounding the pundits of the day - provided the springboard for the development of lengthy narrow gauge systems throughout Britain, the Empire and eventually the world. Selecting a mere 22 postcards of the Welsh narrow gauge, out of literally thousands known to have been published, proved to be a difficult task, as even with only the author's relatively limited collection to choose from, over 20 cards had to be rejected for each one published!

This volume, then, is devoted exclusively to Wales: or at least the area north of a line Aberystwyth—Shrewsbury, the scope for narrow gauge exploration in South Wales being severely limited (though not entirely absent). The field surveyed is that of the entire range of postcard publishing: 'commercial' postcards produced by national or regional publishers, and local photographers; 'enthusiast' photographic cards produced in more limited quantities (and intended to be collected rather than sent through the post); and last but not least 'official' cards produced by or on behalf of the railways concerned.

Even with a whole book devoted to Wales, some selectivity is needed to keep the subject manageable, so we have restricted our survey to railways of 15in gauge and above, and have imposed a 'cut-off' date of 1965. This allows us to include some views of the F.R., T.R. and W.L.L.R. in early 'preservation' days, an era itself now a matter of historical research, and the views we have selected, as well as showing the ongoing development of postcard design, provide a fascinating contrast with earlier 'working' days on these Railways. This cut-off inevitably dictates exclusion of the later generation of tourist railways, such as the Llanberis Lake and Bala Lake, but it is pleasing to note that these new lines have been quick to exploit the publicity and revenue-earning potential of the picture postcard, with some attractive examples already issued. We have also greatly increased our coverage of industrial narrow gauge lines, in recognition of the important role these railways played in the development of the industrial and transport infrastructure of the region.

In writing the captions we have assumed (at least) a basic knowledge of each public Railway's characteristics and history: for those wishing to know more a Select Bibliography is provided (page 55). Spelling of place names follows the style generally in use during the period surveyed: this means that 'anglicised' versions of names such as Portmadoc, Towyn, etc. are used in preference to the Welsh forms officially encouraged from the 1970's onwards.

Finally our previous 'postcard' books have been written with the postcard collector and retailer in mind, with detailed information about postcard types, publication dates, 'checklists' of serial numbers, values, etc. Regrettably our concern for the peculiar requirements of these groups has not been rewarded by significant sales to collectors, and support from the postcard 'Trade' has been disappointing. So in the circumstances checklists have been dropped from this volume, and the space thus released devoted to extra pictures. Nevertheless we have included the name of each postcard's publisher (where known), any omissions being due to either a desire for anonymity on the part of the original publisher, or the fact that we have been obliged to work from later copies not bearing the publisher's imprint.

* *7¼" Gauge News*

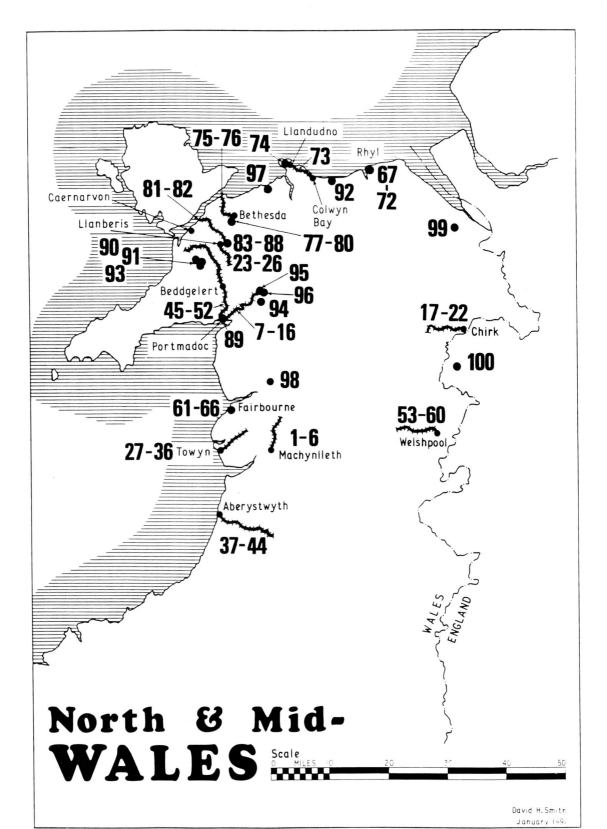

North & Mid-
WALES

Scale
0 MILES 10 20 30 40 50

David H. Smith
January 1991

CORRIS RAILWAY

1

Like the Festiniog (its earlier predecessor) the Corris Railway began life as a horse tramway linking slate quarries in the hills with the nearest navigable waterway, and again passenger carrying and steam traction came later. Opened on 30 April 1859 to a gauge of 2ft 3in the western end of the line to a quay at Derwenlas on the River Dovey was rendered redundant only five years later when the standard gauge railway was completed through Machynlleth and it became more economic to tranship slate to rail there. Following a takeover by Bristol Tramways in 1879 steam locomotives were introduced, the line rebuilt to suit them, and a passenger service introduced in 1883, although passengers had been carried unofficially for some years before. Henry Hughes of Loughborough built three 0-4-0ST but after they had proved unstable on the sharp curves all three were rebuilt with a rear pony truck in the 1890's. These two cards published by Morgan, Photographer (Abergynolwyn) show (1) No. 2 about to leave the upper terminus at Aberllefeni about 1902 and (2) the same or a similar train at Llwyngwern station. The line in the foreground is the short branch to Llwyngwern slate quarry, now well known as the site of the National Centre for Alternative Technology.

2

Corris Toy Train

FFRIDD WOOD, CORRIS RAILWAY. 338

The Corris Railway's new English owners appointed J. R. Dix, a 27 year old ex Cambrian Railways man as General Manager, and for nearly 30 years he ran the line in a most capable manner, making every effort to attract traffic, taking any and all opportunities to publicise the line and producing a steady dividend for his shareholders. One example of his flair for publicity was encouraging the production of postcards, by the Railway itself and by 'commercial' firms.   (3) is a card by D. S. George and Son, showing an up train passing through Ffridd Woods about ¾ mile from Machynlleth. In a guidebook Dix eloquently described this as "exactly resembling the Queen's Drive at Balmoral"! (4) For much of the route between Machynlleth and Corris the railway ran alongside the main road, leaving it at Maesporth then running through open country to Corris, the main intermediate station. This was an impressive affair with an overall roof, signal cabin, carriage shed and coal yard. This F. Moores card shows the station from the south end with the carriage shed centre and coal siding to the right. A railway bus, harbinger of the line's eventual demise, lurks at the far end of the station.

7196

(5) By 1920 all three steam locomotives were badly worn and No. 3 was given a complete rebuild. However as No. 1 had been written off completely and No. 2 was little better the Railway bought a new locomotive the following year. No. 4 was a slightly modified version of Kerr, Stuart's standard 'Tattoo' class 0-4-2ST and is depicted on an F. Moores card – its slight blemishes hopefully outweighed by the interest of the subject – taking water by the loco shed at Maesporth. There was no station here but passengers were expected to wait patiently in their seats while the loco took water and coal (by passing out baskets through the adjoining shed window!) or even ambled off to shunt any wagons for the horse worked branch to Upper Corris.   (6) Through the 1920's road competition and a declining slate industry hit the line hard, and eventually the whole railway was sold to the G.W.R. for a mere £1,000 in 1930. They promptly withdrew passenger trains, scrapped Nos. 1 and 2 and the carriages, but maintained a daily freight service – depicted here on an anonymous photographic card – and promoted this with some success initially. But when flooding of the River Dovey cut the line in 1948 the inevitable end came, although fortunately the two locos and some stock survived to be bought by the Talyllyn Railway in 1951.

FESTINIOG RAILWAY

7

In its early years the Festiniog Railway was not just a minor Welsh narrow gauge railway but a tremendous influence on railway development worldwide, not only by proving that such a narrow gauge as two feet could move significant loads and that practical steam locomotives could be built to haul them, but in its pioneering work with the articulated locomotive and the bogie coach. (7) is an early (1871) scene at Portmadoc, reproduced over the years by various publishers, with the pioneering 1869 Fairlie LITTLE WONDER posed with all four types of original 4 wheel coaches. Note the 'T' railed track still in use in the foreground and the original goods shed behind the train.   (8) The long awaited opening of the Welsh Highland Railway in 1923 was coupled with a wave of optimism and publicity, and this view is believed to have been specially set up for Photochrom's photographer, Mr. Bucknall. The Davies brothers pose with Robert Evans, then F.R. Manager, on PALMERSTON in Portmadoc (Harbour) platform. Note the Fairlie loco backing on to the front end, to power the train back across the 'Cob' afterwards.

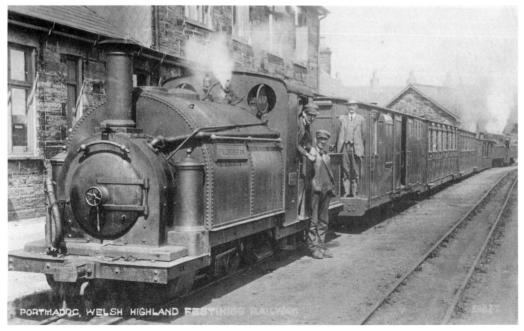

PORTMADOC, WELSH HIGHLAND FESTINIOG RAILWAY.

8

(9) TALIESIN a 'single Fairlie' 0-4-4T built by Vulcan Foundry in 1876 was very similar in design to the pair Vulcan had built for the North Wales Narrow Gauge Railway two years earlier but with the driving bogie dimensions of the F.R.'s previous 'double Fairlie' built by Avonside in 1872. This LPC card shows her posed at Boston Lodge sometime after her major rebuild of 1898-1900 when reboiled and given a new cab. Highly regarded as a fast and economical all purpose engine she nevertheless died a lingering death at Boston Lodge in the depressed conditions of the early 1930's. (10) First station out of Portmadoc was Minffordd, an important interchange with the Cambrian Railways and consequently meriting an imposing station building, erected in 1887. Despite its picturesque setting, it was relatively neglected by postcard publishers: this is one of the few known examples, probably a Friths card, depicting a short train for Blaenau behind an England engine. It will be noted from this (and the following view of Tan-y-Bwlch) that F.R. trains adopted right-hand running at loops, contrary to traditional British practice. Gravity-operated slate trains – often running at high speed to gain momentum for the crossing of the 'Cob' – ran through the line on the right.

FESTINIOG RAILWAY, MINFFORDD.

11

(11) Two passenger trains cross at Tan-y-Bwylch about 1875 – depicted on a tinted 'commercial' card published some years later. The second double Fairlie JAMES SPOONER, built by Avonside in 1872, is on the down train on the left. Note the station then had a middle road which was removed in 1896; also the distinctive 'curly roof' brake on the up train, one of the original trio of bogie brake vans. (12) A photographic card from the inter-War period when the F.R. was relatively neglected by 'commercial' publishers, barring the statutory posed pictures of Station Mistresses in Welsh costume at Tan-y-Bwylch! TALIESIN has brought its train from Portmadoc into the 'G.W.R.' station at Blaenau Festiniog; most of the passengers have drifted off to catch a main line connection or to sample the delights of Blaenau on a rainy afternoon, but one father stays behind for a chat with the loco crew. This rather youthful pair are happy to pause for a while and 'tell the tale' to father and son (or daughter?). This location has now radically changed, following the construction of the F.R.'s new interchange station with B.R. in the 1980's.

12

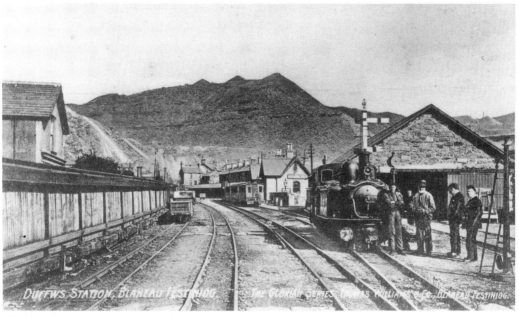

(13) The eastern terminus of the F.R. proper was at Duffws, seen here on a 'Glorian series' card by local publisher Thomas Williams & Co. JAMES SPOONER poses with crew before running round, circa 1905. In the centre background is the line up to Votty and Bowydd slate quarries, whose towering waste tips still dominate the Blaenau skyline today. A second incline curved sharply around to the Festiniog Mineral Extension. By means of several inclines and locomotive worked sections this served first the Maenofferen Quarry and then Cwt-y-Bugail, Manod and ultimately Rhiwbach slate quarries. Duffws closed to passenger traffic on 31 May 1931 and thereafter was used purely as a yard for marshalling slate traffic. Today the site is a car park but the station building continues to serve the public as a 'convenience'. (14) In 1879 and 1885 Boston Lodge completed two more double Fairlie locomotives generally similar to JAMES SPOONER. The first was named MERDDIN EMRYS and the second LIVINGSTON THOMPSON, inheriting the name TALIESIN from the single Fairlie when that was withdrawn in 1931. Like most F.R. engines it has been much rebuilt over the years but is seen here in virtually 'as built' condition about 1900.

Festiniog Toy Railway

15

Reviving the F.R. proved to be a more demanding task than had confronted the first group of preservationists, at Towyn, a few years before. Not only had the F.R. been closed since 1946, suffering the depredations of weather and vandals, but there was also a morass of legal obstacles to surmount. Years of negotiation culminated in the new Company taking over in 1954. (15) Initially it was only possible to repair the track as far as Boston Lodge, and a shuttle service powered by the Simplex petrol 'tractor' ran between there and Portmadoc for about 10 days in July 1955. It is seen here entering Boston Lodge. Absence of a run-round loop meant the carriages had to be hand- or chain-shunted, a possible explanation for the pole being flourished by the crewman. (16) PRINCE returned to service on 2 August 1955 and between then and September 1956 worked all traffic until reinforced by the double Fairlie TALIESIN. In 1956, services were extended to Minffordd, and up to six return workings ran each day. This pleasing study by Friths – one of the few 'Edwardian' era publishers to continue producing cards in the 1950's and 60's – depicts PRINCE awaiting departure from Portmadoc.

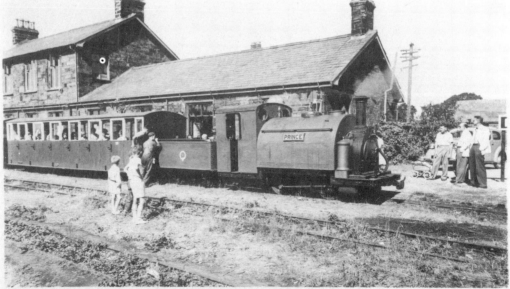

PTMC.94T.   PORTMADOC TOY RAILWAY.   Copyright Frith Ltd

16

GLYN VALLEY TRAMWAY

Pontfaen Station, Glyn Valley Tramway   *'The Unique Series'*

Roadside steam tramways were never as common in Britain as in Continental Europe but mid Wales had one, the Glyn Valley Tramway, which ran westwards from Chirk up the lovely Ceirog valley to bring roadstone and slate from quarries above Glyn Ceirog, 8½ miles away, with a further three mile mineral extension down to Hendre granite quarry. Opened as a horse tramway in April 1873, passenger traffic began a year later. The gauge was originally 2ft 4¼in (exactly half standard gauge) but when reconstructed in the mid 1880's as a locomotive worked line, this was widened by ¼in, allowing better clearance on the sharp curves. The Railway was very much a common carrier, moving slate and stone east for transhipment to the G.W.R. at Chirk, coal inwards and a reasonably healthy passenger and general merchandise traffic, at least at first. Motive power was originally three delightful Beyer Peacock 0-4-2 side tanks, fitted with side covers over their wheels and motion as the law demanded. One is seen (17) on a tinted card in the 'Unique' series, posed at Pontfaen crossing circa 1909 with a mixed train for Glyn Ceirog. In the lower view (18) GLYN, the third and last of the trio, pauses for the photographer at Glyn Ceirog about 1926, before backing on to its train for the return journey.

THE STATION, GLYNCEIRIOG.

(19) Facilities at Glyn Ceirog were quite lavish by narrow gauge standards with a loco shed and turntable, and sidings for coal, timber and general freight. The railway divided here, passenger trains taking the left fork which continued beyond the passenger station for three miles up the valley to Hendre, whilst the line to the right ran past the loco shed and across the road to finish at inclines to the Wynne and Cambrian slate quarries, as can be clearly seen in our upper view, again a tinted card in the 'Unique' series, the publisher of which is identified only as 'B&C'. (20) On another commercial card, SIR THEODORE has run round and is about to return to Chirk. Following the familiar pattern, an initial period of moderate prosperity gradually faded into mounting losses after World War 1. First the slump hit the slate trade, then after 1924 bus competition began to eat into the passenger traffic, and even the Railway's main revenue source, the Ceirog Granite Co., began to use lorries. Passenger traffic finally ceased on 6 April 1933 but for another two years the line tried hard to survive on freight alone, before finally closing on 6 July 1935.

TRAIN LEAVING STATION.

20

(21) By 1920 SIR THEODORE needed major repairs, and to help out DENNIS and GLYN the G.V.T. purchased a War surplus 60cm gauge Baldwin 4-6-0T from the dump at Purfleet, Essex, the first of several U.K. narrow gauge railways to do so. It was sent to Beyer Peacock in January 1921 who made a beautiful if expensive job of overhauling and regauging it, including the provision of a nice copper capped chimney. Despite this facelift it was never popular, mainly being confined to freight duties. Depicted on a 'Real Photographs' card standing on the shed road at Chirk, it makes an interesting contrast with GLYN. (22) About 1926 some thought was given to converting GLYN to a Sentinel vertical boilered geared steam loco, following the example set by a number of owners of small standard gauge industrial steam locomotives. But by this time cash and time were running out, and SIR THEODORE had at last had a major overhaul at the makers, so the need was not really there. As far as possible SIR THEODORE was latterly used on passenger trains and our final view shows it crossing the road at Glyn Ceirog, whilst running round its train.

SNOWDON MOUNTAIN RAILWAY

Llanberis Station, Snowdon Railway

The Snowdon Mountain Railway is Wales' (and Britain's) only example of the 'rack and pinion' railway. 1991 sees its 95th year of operation, a period during which it has seen remarkably little alteration. One loss however has been the original (1896) Llanberis station building, built largely of wood in a 'Swiss chalet' style, and later replaced by a more conventional brick structure. The direction of the sun makes photography of the station difficult, consequently postcards of it from this viewpoint are relatively scarce: (23) was issued as a sepia card in the 'Kingsway' real photographic series (S8595). (24) Switzerland being the home of the 'rack and pinion' railway, it was not surprising that the Snowdon company placed their orders for locomotives with the Swiss Locomotive and Machine Co., Winterthur, the acknowledged experts in this specialised field who supplied five locomotives to their typical Abt rack system designed in 1895-6 and a further three with small side tanks in 1922-3. From 1959 Hunslet have undertaken much rebuilding of these locos, finally breaking the steam monopoly by supplying two new diesel locos in 1986.

(25) Clogwyn Station, 3½ miles out and just over 2,200 feet up, is the last passing place on the S.M.R. In very bad weather trains terminate here for the final section is not only the most exposed but also the worst climb, nearly 1,000 feet in less than a mile. One problem for photographers is the uncertainty of the weather –however sunny the day on the lower slopes Snowdon summit may often be wreathed in cloud. Luckily H. Gordon Tidey has picked a particularly fine day for his visit about 1926 and the passengers are taking a breather while waiting to pass another train. This fine card was produced by Lens of Sutton, who specialise in RP cards of locomotives, trains and stations. (26) Although the S.M.R. has always been a popular subject for postcards the railway is very often just a small part of an overall view and good close up cards of Summit Station are rare. This is a pleasant 1950's commercial card of a train arriving at Summit. The final grade into the station is amongst the steepest on the entire railway as can just be seen on the left of the picture, while behind the platform is the footpath to the summit itself.

TAL-Y-LLYN RAILWAY

27

The Talyllyn Railway has achieved considerable fame both as one of the oldest passenger carrying narrow gauge lines and as the pioneer of enthusiast run railways worldwide. Opened for passenger and freight in 1866 and steam worked from the start it brought slate down the Afon Fathew valley from Bryn Eglwys slate quarry high up on Cader Idris to the coastal main line at Towyn. Like its neighbour the Corris Railway its gauge was 2ft 3in. A remarkable feature of the line was the virtual complete absence of change from its opening, to the preservation society's takeover in 1951. Having built a railway and bought two locomotives, four carriages, a brake and some goods wagons to operate it, that was that! It not only escaped the Grouping and Nationalisation but also such tedious trivia as filing annual Ministry returns, and troubling an insurance company to inspect the locomotive boilers. Numerous publishers, local and national, produced cards of the railway over the years: our first two views are undated but probably from the 1920's. (27) is a Harvey Barton and Sons sepia card depicting TALYLLYN awaiting departure from Towyn (Wharf). (28) is a 'real photo' card by the prolific publisher Raphael Tuck, showing DOLGOCH – with locally added cab door – after arrival at Wharf.

28

TWN 10   *Tal-y-Llyn Railway, Towyn*   *A Tuck Card*

(29) Fletcher Jennings were one of the earliest 'mainstream' locomotive builders to design locomotives specifically for industrial and narrow gauge railways, supplying several saddle tanks of between 2ft 8in and 4ft 8½in gauge for South Wales iron works in the early 1860's. The T.R.'s first locomotive TAL-Y-LLYN was very much to this pattern but their second was radically different, being built to Fletcher's Patent design. As applied to the 2ft 3in gauge DOLGOCH the rear overhang is reduced by placing the rear axle behind the firebox and driving the valve gear off the front axle with the water carried in both a well tank and a tank at the rear. Our early 1930's view shows her – temporarily running nameless – posed at Wharf Station, on a divided back photographic card by Real Photos (Liverpool). (30) In pre-preservation days TAL-Y-LLYN was more popular with the staff and is seen here posed with a short passenger train near Pentremaestrefnant approaching Abergynolwyn terminus. As the loco carries its second saddle tank the picture was taken some time before 1926: it is a Valentine's photo issued (as was a regular practice with this firm) by local photographer George & Sons, and posted in 1935.

31

(31) While the other Welsh railways fortunate enough to still have passenger services operating in 1939 ceased running them on the outbreak of war, the Talyllyn continued to operate a service of some kind throughout the conflict. Initially two trains each way ran on Mondays, Wednesdays and Fridays, though frequency was later reduced as the strains of war added to the existing maintenance backlog. The public were encourage to 'holiday at home' during the War, and enough holidaymakers are present to make up a respectable load for TAL-Y-LLYN as she departs Brynglas with a train for Abergynolwyn on 16 August 1940 (anonymous photographic card, numbered TR9399). (32) The story of how the T.R. became the first railway in the world to be rescued and operated by amateurs attracted widespread media interest in the drab days of 1950, and several Publishers released cards of the first seasons of operation, 1951 and 1952. This is a Salmon 'Photostyle' black and white printed card and may have been published for the Railway: unusually it names the locomotive as well as the Railway and location. Society founder (and General Manager for the first two years) Tom Rolt, in familiar straw hat, is visible behind DOLGOCH.

32   DOLGOCH, TAL-Y-LLYN RAILWAY, TOWYN   20336

Of all the Preservation Societies, the Talyllyn was the most prolific in producing 'official' postcards for fund-raising and publicity purposes. Early issues were of the 'real photo' type, serially numbered in a two-digit series, and are extremely collectable, although not always highly valued by postcard dealers. (33) TR23 was taken from an original by J. C. Flemons and is a charming study of No. 4 EDWARD THOMAS entering Rhydyronen station with the original passenger stock, probably in 1952. Note the short grass grown siding on the right which was used to run DOLGOCH around her stock on the initial re-opening day, Whit Monday 1951, when trains only ran as far as here. (34) Early hopes that the ex Corris Railway No. 3 would relieve the ailing DOLGOCH were dashed when the T.R.'s appalling track derailed SIR HAYDYN (as she was named) at the least excuse. By 1953 enough track maintenance had been completed to allow her to be used – TR 29 shows her passing Quarry Siding with a somewhat mixed train comprising Corris van No. 6, an original T.R. coach, and the two coaches rebuilt from ex Penrhyn workmen's carriages.

35

(35) Another T.R. 'official' postcard (TR25) from the mid-1950's, this study of SIR HAYDYN and train at Abergynolwyn is now a 'period picture' in its own right. Relaying the decrepit run-round loop here was an early Preservation Society priority but otherwise little was changed initially. Nowadays the guard wears a uniform and the station was totally rebuilt in 1968-69. It now has a smart new building of traditional style and materials but more significantly trains now continue on up the re-opened mineral extension to Nant Gwernol. (36) The T.R. gained a fifth steam locomotive in 1953 which, like No. 4, was an 'off the peg' maker's standard design. One of six modified 'E' class 0-4-0WT built by Andrew Barclay for airfield construction work during 1918 it spent most of its military life on the RAF railway at Calshot, near Southampton, being generously donated to the T.R. by Messrs Abelson of Birmingham who had purchased her on the Calshot Railway's closure in 1945. Having been rebuilt from 2ft gauge and named DOUGLAS after a Director of Abelson's, she has become a valuable member of the T.R.'s fleet, and has managed to maintain the Talyllyn tradition of mechanical longevity by still retaining her original boiler. ('official' card, TR30.)

36

VALE OF RHEIDOL RAILWAY

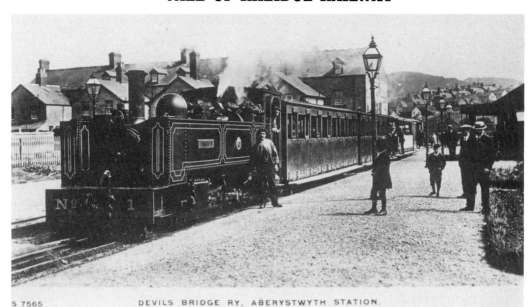

37

The 1ft 11½in gauge Vale of Rheidol Railway is now under its fifth ownership, having started as an independent Company, been taken over by the Cambrian in 1910, absorbed by the G.W.R. in 1922, nationalised in 1948, and in 1988 returned to the Private Sector. The VOR Co.'s original Aberystwyth terminus was pleasant and spacious, with flower beds and a generous allocation of acetylene gas lamps, but only a ground level 'platform'. (37) is a superb view of the station, issued as a sepia card in the 'Kingsway' series (S7565). The picture dates from the year of the Cambrian takeover, but the only immediate change is No. 1's livery, a two-tone green with black banding round the tanks, separated by pale cream lining. No. 1 EDWARD VII and No. 2 PRINCE OF WALES were two identical 2-6-2T's built by the Romiley firm, Davies and Metcalfe in 1902. (38) shows a train in pre-Cambrian days at a rarely-photographed location, on the approach to Devil's Bridge; the building on the right is an old woollen mill, and the single storey building behind the fence is the contractor's navvy barracks, purchased from the Elan Valley reservoir contract (sepia card, unknown publisher).

38

23

(39) The VOR's No. 3, RHEIDOL was the 'odd man out' in the locomotive fleet, being a Bagnall 2-4-0T of their type 'Jessie' with outside frames and Baguley valve gear. Works No. 1497, she was ordered in June 1896 as a 750mm gauge loco for plantation service in Brazil. However the order was cancelled and, regauged to 2ft 3in, she was sold the following year to the remote Plynlimon and Hafan Tramway in the hills north of Aberystwyth. When that short lived and unhappy concern gave up the ghost in 1900 Bagnalls bought her back from the liquidator, regauged her yet again to 1ft 11½in and sold her to Pethick Bros. for building the VOR. Work completed, she became the VOR's No. 3, being intended purely for shunting. She is seen carrying her original spark arrestor chimney at Aberystwyth about 1903. (40) In pre-G.W.R. days freight, primarily mineral ores, timber and cattle was an important part of the VOR's business, but due to road competition this ceased at the end of 1926. A mixed train is seen at Rheidol Falls Halt about this time.

S 7566   *Devil's Bridge Railway, Devil's Bridge Station*

(41) Whatever the intentions regarding RHEIDOL (see (39)), small narrow gauge companies like the VOR couldn't afford the luxury of pure shunting locos. With the Railway's chronic motive power shortage, the little Bagnall was soon being thrashed up to Devil's Bridge and back, usually twice sometimes three times a day on regular passenger duties. Heavy repairs at the end of 1904 included a conventional chimney and as such she is seen at Devil's Bridge terminus about 1906. As can be seen in this Kingsway card, the original station was a very basic affair in the best light railway timber and corrugated iron tradition, although in 1904 there were sufficient funds to add the two 'lean to' toilets on the end of the station building.   (42) is another early commercial card, a variant of the familiar view looking down from the footbridge on top of the cutting at the station throat. Note the spare coach in the siding, which along with any loaded wagons from the two freight sidings just out of the left of the picture, will be added to the last train of the day down to Aberystwyth. This timeless scene is little changed today, apart from the addition of some 'commercial' buildings over to the left of the now superfluous goods yard.

43

(43) The VOR's consultant engineer Sir James Szlumper and his half brother William had previously occupied similar positions during the construction of the Lynton and Barnstaple Railway. They based their design for the VOR locos on the L. & B. machines but with a shorter wheelbase, smaller driving wheels and a better designed boiler. The end result may not have been so aesthetically pleasing as the Devon locos but produced a highly successful locomotive with the power to slog up the line's nearly four miles of 1 in 50 with an 80 ton train. Davies and Metcalfe of Romily near Stockport secured the order for the first two locos EDWARD VII and PRINCE OF WALES and did a first class job. However by the time the G.W.R. took over both badly needed supplementing, so Swindon set to and built two similar locomotives but with many detail differences. They were numbered 7 and 8: the former is seen in Aberystwyth terminus around 1924 on this Real Photos (Broadstairs) card. (44) In 1956 B.R. named them OWAIN GLYNDWYR and LLEWELLYN respectively and restored the name to PRINCE OF WALES, the surviving original engine (the other had been scrapped in 1935). Carrying the then current B.R. logo on the tank sides PRINCE OF WALES and crew pose for the photographer at Aberystwyth about 1959.

44

WELSH HIGHLAND RAILWAY

45

Unfulfilled dreams . . . In June 1923 a through route was at last opened from Portmadoc to the north as the Welsh Highland Railway – a new company formed to combine the North Wales Narrow Gauge Railway and the Portmadoc, Beddgelert and South Snowdon, a grandiose title that contrasted sharply with virtually no achievements. Fond hopes of a narrow gauge El Dorado soon faded into Welsh mist as losses steadily rose amidst endless bickering among almost everyone involved. Just south of the crossing over the G.W.R. at Portmadoc the 'New' station was built – a simple affair with a passing loop, low platform and corrugated iron shelter. Working of the W.H.R. was closely linked with the Festiniog and in this 1923 commercial card (45) a George England engine waits at the platform.   (46) By 1934 the effects of road competition and the economic slump had reduced traffic to the point where closure was inevitable but at the last moment the F.R. took a lease. As part of a hurried 'spring clean' of locos and stock the ex-War Department Baldwin 4-6-0T was repaired and fitted with a wooden cab backsheet. In this form it is pictured on a Friths card hauling a train through the spectacular Aberglaslyn pass.

Welsh Highland Railway in Aberglaslyn Pass

46

47   *Beddgelert Station, Welsh Highland Railway*

One effect of the W.H.R.'s internal squabbles was that it was never really worked as one railway. Beddgelert became the 'frontier station', north of here coming under the control of D. O. Jones, the long-suffering station master at Dinas Junction, but from here south was regarded as the Festiniog's responsibility, whatever management or the timetable might say. Although trains, at least at first, worked right through, they usually dawdled for an hour or so at Beddgelert, as if to ensure that any passenger optimistic enough to book a through journey did not repeat the mistake twice. Later it was actually necessary to change trains. This Friths card (47) however dates from 1923 when all was fresh and new, not excluding the bookstall (just in view, right) where – who knows? – this postcard may have been purchased by a hopeful passenger. An F. R. England engine has uncoupled from its train to run forward and take water before continuing to Dinas. (48) is another card from this early period and again shows an England engine and F.R. train, about to leave Dinas Junction. Only the barest minimum of renovation work was done to the original N.W.N.G.R. trackwork as part of the W.H.R. construction contract, creating yet more problems for the handful of overworked staff to contend with.

48

(49) In 1908 the N.W.N.G.R. bought GOWRIE, their third single Fairlie 0-6-4T, vainly hoping that their Portmadoc extension would finally be built. Built by Hunslet it differed from its older Vulcan Foundry sisters in many details, including outside Walschaert's valve gear, larger cylinders and a smaller boiler. The latter, plus the lengthy steam pipes inherent in the design, were probably responsible for its reputation as a poor steamer. With a much reduced service during World War 1 it could easily be spared and the opportunity was seized to dump it on the Government at a War inflated price. What use, if any, they made of it is unknown, but it was employed later on an aerodrome construction contract in Yorkshire, disappearing, presumed scrapped, after 1928. This Preservation Society card, published about 1964, shows it at Quellyn Lake pre-War.   (50) The W.H.R.'s boss after 1923, the redoubtable Colonel Stephens, was a keen purchaser of ex military equipment for all his light railways, and this included a number of ex W.D.L.R. Baldwin 4-6-0T's from France. The Welsh Highland got one, which retained its military number to the end, and is depicted on an F. Moores divided back postcard at Dinas Junction, circa 1923. An extended cab roof and vacuum brake have already been added.

51

Contributions to the War Effort . . . (51) In February 1917 the by now freight only N.W.N.G.R. was used to test the first three Dick, Kerr petrol electric locos built for trench tramway use in France. This then novel design was the origin from which the ubiquitous B.R. '08' diesel shunter was ultimately derived. A Dick, Kerr stands alongside RUSSELL at Dinas Junction exchange sidings, the latter in steam for the irregular freight service. This would include pit prop timber from south of Rhyd-ddu, brought to there by an ex Glanrafon Quarry DeWinton working over temporary track on the incomplete P.B.S.S.R. formation (see (45) above). (52) The W.H.R.'s part in World War 2 was much sadder, if inevitable. Having finally closed in June 1937 its derelict track and stock were requisitioned for scrap and demolition by Cohen's began in August 1941. The contractors brought in two Hibberd petrol locos, rebuilt from ex W.D.L.R. 40hp Simplexes, to haul the demolition trains. Fortunately the job was recorded photographically by J. F. Bolton and one such scrap train is shown here, posed somewhere above Beddgelert. Both views on this page are taken from postcards published by the present W.H.R. as part of a series of historic views.

52

WELSHPOOL AND LLANFAIR RAILWAY

53

The 2ft 6in gauge Welshpool and Llanfair Light Railway was the last 'new' public narrow gauge line to be built in Wales, opening in 1904. If differed from its predecessors in having no staple slate or mineral traffic, instead being a true 'common carrier', connecting the market town of Welshpool with the agricultural hinterland. Relative to the other Welsh railways it was neglected by postcard publishers, (53) is one of only a handful of known views of the terminus at Llanfair Caerinion. Published by Valentine's of Dundee, it depicts Beyer Peacock 0-6-0T THE EARL, in original condition, on a mixed train from Welshpool. Features of interest include the very basic waiting shelter and the station nameboard reading simply 'Llanfair'. (54) The crossing of a town centre street by narrow gauge passenger trains was unusual even in Edwardian days, so it is not surprising that cards depicting trains negotiating the Union Street level crossing in Welshpool appear under the imprint of several publishers, and in both sepia and tinted versions. This example, again by Valentine's, is postally used in 1911, but the view dates from c.1904. Despite the usual shortage of cash, the W. & L. purchased three quite impressive bogie coaches from R. Y. Pickering & Co. of Glasgow, which are clearly seen here.

54

55

(55) Postcards of freight trains are extremely rare, so we are fortunate that L.P.C. made available this fine real photograph of a goods working at Welshpool in their 'Locomotive Magazine' series (L989). The W. & L. had to work hard for its freight, the only staple traffic being house coal, livestock to and from Welshpool market, plus considerable quantities of timber in earlier years. The photo is almost certainly taken in pre Great War days and shows 0-6-0T THE EARL shunting some of the batch of 4 wheel bolster wagons built by Pickerings in 1904.

(56) This interesting Real Photographs (Southport) view of COUNTESS in Welshpool yard was presumably taken soon after the G.W.R. takeover on 1 January 1923. Note that the loco has now acquired G.W.R. 823 numberplates and has had its nameplate moved to the cab side, necessitating cutting the word 'THE' from it, but still retains its original Ramsbottom safety valves. When the locomotive was reboilered at Swindon in July 1930 it also gained a much larger steam dome, copper cap chimney, top feed and the inevitable Swindon brass trumpet casing over the safety valves.

56

Remarkably, even during an era when numerous conventional branch lines were closing each year, British Railways allowed the W.L.L.R. to pursue its unhurried – and surely unremunerative – life, carrying a dwindling amount of freight between Welshpool and Llanfair for a full eight years after Nationalisation. Increasing recognition of the line's status as a state-run anachronism attracted numerous photographers during the 1950's. (57) On 25 June 1954 823 shunts its train in the exchange sidings by Welshpool station. The somewhat cramped yard here included a stretch of mixed gauge track, a little of which survives in use today. (58) The usual consist of a W. & L. freight train in the 1950's would be about six wagons – coal, fertilizer and some general goods for Llanfair, but only the odd wagon load of wool back. Presumably this undated view, issued as a Photomatic card, was taken on market day, for the train is up to the permitted maximum of 14 empty wagons. By now the locomotive carried number plates only, the nameplates having been removed for safe keeping in March 1951.

(59) When it became obvious that B.R. intended to close the line, a number of enthusiast 'specials' were run, utilising station seats placed in open wagons for 'coaching stock'. Such trips would be hugely oversubscribed today, but things were different then, one 1955 special being so poorly supported that the Station Master at Welshpool persuaded his family to augment the numbers. Even so the trains provided valuable publicity for attempts being made to preserve the line, and views of various trains were published as postcards.   (60) One early priority for the line's new owners was to acquire some suitable coaching stock, the original fleet having been scrapped at Swindon in 1936, when thoughts of rebuilding them for the Vale of Rheidol were finally abandoned. Fortunately 2ft 6in was the 'standard' gauge for naval armament depot railways, and closure of the Chattenden and Upnor Railway in Kent on 29 May 1961 released a quantity of suitable stock, which arrived at Welshpool that July. On this early Preservation Society 'official' card COUNTESS arrives at Cyfronydd with a train of C. & U.R. stock, consisting of the 4 wheel brake, two semi-open toastrack coaches, a third rebuilt by the W. & L. with doors, and the 'Combination Car' at the rear.

FAIRBOURNE RAILWAY

Bassett-Lowke Miniature Railway at Fairbourne (Wales)

The Fairbourne Railway dates – as a 15in gauge operation – from 1916 when W. J. Bassett-Lowke's company Narrow Gauge Railways Ltd. regauged and extended an earlier horse-drawn tramway. (61) a Bassett-Lowke 'official' postcard shows 'Little Giant' 4-4-2 PRINCE EDWARD OF WALES at 'old Bathing Beach Halt' circa 1916, posed with a typical train of Bassett-Lowke 'opens; which make no concession to the North Wales climate! Note the initials 'NGR' on No. 22's tender. The bell tents in the background were temporarily used as changing cubicles prior to the erection of chalets in the 1920's. (62) is a R.A. series black and white printed card, showing the same loco and train posed at the original ferry terminus. This was completely washed away, along with a quarter of a mile of track, in the storm of October 1927. This view can be precisely dated to 1921-22, as during the 1921 coal strike the engines had to burn wood, and additional screens and awnings were fitted, as the small end screens shown in the preceding view were insufficient protection against the sparks thrown off by the engine. No. 22's tender now proclaims 'F M R' (Fairbourne Miniature Railway) as Narrow Gauge Railways Ltd. were no longer in existence. The driver (in white cap) is Stanley Harrison.

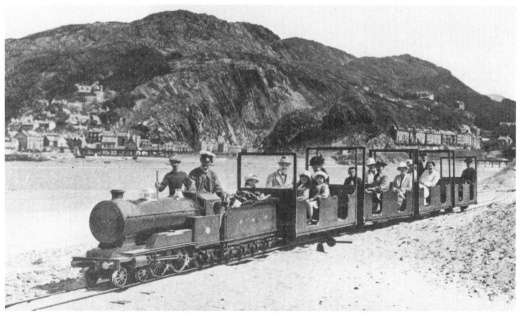

Fairbourne Miniature Railway

63

Miniature train at Barmouth Ferry Terminus

219320 J.V.

(63) After the 1927 flood referred to in illus. 62, the line was cut back and in 1933 was diverted to this temporary terminus on the landward side of the peninsular. There was only a siding here, no loop, and it was a further five years before the line was extended back to its former terminus. This view, published as a Valentine's sepia card, (Z19320) dates from around 1935 and depicts driver Leslie Vaughton at the controls of COUNT LOUIS, another 'Little Giant', built for use on a private railway at Highams Park owned by Count Louis Zbrowski, but never used there due to the Count's death in 1924. (64) The F.R. management were early enthusiasts for the use of internal combustion locomotives, purchasing a Lister 'Rail Truck' 4 wheel petrol loco in April 1935. This was a standard industrial locomotive design powered by a JAP air cooled engine and was primarily used to haul the first and last trains of the day. In this L.C.G.B. Ken Nunn card the Lister, manned by a somewhat youthful crew, leaves Fairbourne with a rake of Bassett-Lowke 'opens'. After the War the Lister was joined by a second similar loco rebuilt from 2ft gauge and gained the name WHIPPIT QUICK.

64

While postcard coverage of some Welsh railways virtually ceased between the 1930's and mid-1950's, we are fortunate that all stages of the F.R.'s development are documented on postcards. (65) is a most interesting 1948 view depicting COUNT LOUIS, as rebuilt in 1946/47, at Penrhyn Bridge, just to the north of the temporary terminus depicted in illus. 63. The first three vehicles are all steel coaches, built by the Railway's new owners Wilkins and Mitchell (who published this card under the name W&M) in 1948. The driver is Ralph Broom, responsible for COUNT LOUIS' rebuilding. (66) an undated photographic card, shows the final stages of the Railway's development, the commodious new station (right background) having been constructed in 1957-58. Piles of rail to the right of the second coach suggest major track renewals in progress, but sadly all this new investment did not stave off eventual closure in 1985. (The railway has, of course, since been revitalised as a new 12¼in gauge operation, using the trackbed, but little else, of the original Railway). The locomotive is ERNEST W. TWINING, a freelance Pacific originally from the Dudley Zoo Railway.

RHYL MINIATURE RAILWAY

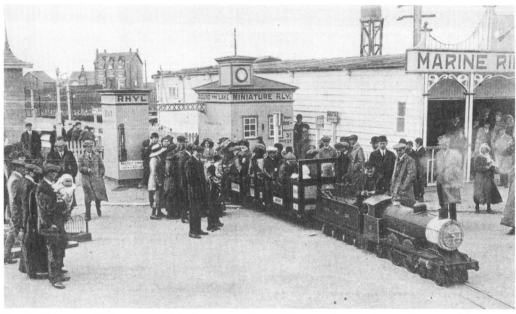

The Rhyl Miniature Railway is one of the longest established fifteen-inch gauge lines in Britain, celebrating its 80th Anniversary in 1991. It is now the oldest miniature railway site still operating with steam. Under the auspices of miniature locomotive builder W. J. Bassett-Lowke, with Henry Greenly as engineer, the railway opened on 1st May 1911 at the Marine Lake, Rhyl, a site already well established for bathing and boating.

(67) Greenly's confident and impressive station design is seen here to good effect on an 'Aerotype Reproduction' tinted card published by local firm Rae Pickard. Our card is postally used in 1912, but the admiring crowds – to whom the railway is clearly a fascinating novelty – suggest that the view may date from the opening season in 1911. Looked at from this angle, the small size of the 'true scale' fifteen inch models is readily apparent. (68) W. J. Bassett-Lowke, a keen photographer, realised the publicity value of picture postcards and published views of various of his railways and locomotives. This example, a sepia card, depicts the first locomotive used at Rhyl, one of the classic 'Little Giant' 4-4-2's, designed by Greenly and built by Bassett-Lowke at Northampton. This locomotive handled all traffic at Rhyl during the 1911 and 1912 seasons, working seven days a week with (at peak times) a 15 hour operating day!

Locomotive, "Prince Edward of Wales," Rhyl Miniature Railway.
BASSETT-LOWKE LTD., Builders, London & Northampton.

69

(69) The R.M.R. provided a run of almost a mile and with passenger traffic increasing, extra locomotive power was needed. In 1913 reinforcements arrived in the shape of a second 'Little Giant' GEORGE THE FIFTH from the Southport Miniature Railway. One of the pair is seen here – probably in 1919 or 1920 – on an unusual card commemorating the exploits of Inspector Waterfield. This seems to have been a subject of interest well outside Rhyl, the photo appearing under the imprint of several publishers, this example being a printed black and white card by Hines of Sunderland.   (70) From 1913 the General Manager of the Rhyl M.R. was Albert Barnes: he concluded that, in terms of the sustained operation with heavy loads required at Rhyl, the 'true scale' Bassett-Lowke locos were underpowered. Henry Greenly therefore designed a development of the class, with larger cylinders and strengthened motion, capable of hauling 80 or more passengers. Construction was undertaken at Albert Barnes' own works in Rhyl, the first example No. 101 JOAN being delivered in 1920. Soon the 'Barnes' locos were in charge of all traffic, this Valentine's card depicts one of the class and a well filled train of Bassett-Lowke stock c.1930. The railway had a circular route, so passengers were always able to 'face the engine'.

MINIATURE TRAIN. MARINE LAKE. RHYL.

70

71

Greenly's 1911 station, attractive though it was, included no wet weather protection for passengers, so was replaced after a few years with a more functional building with overall roof, its architects taking a realistic view of the vagaries of the North Wales weather! (71) This station is seen to good effect on a black and white printed card (W828), one of a series published by Valentines, who were based at Dundee but whose photographers travelled extensively in search of subjects, and made a speciality of miniature railway views. (72) Some time after World War 2 the station was rebuilt yet again, this time in concrete. Valentines again are responsible for this unusual interior view (postally used in 1947), an interesting feature of which is the sign giving the fares – Adults 6d, children 3d – only marginally more than the 3d and 2d charged by Bassett-Lowke in 1911! The Bassett-Lowke coaches are still in evidence, but the locomotives are 'Barnes' Atlantics – the original No. 101 having been joined by three more, JOHN, MICHAEL and BILLY, by 1934, and the two 'Little Giants' disposed of to Margate and Skegness.

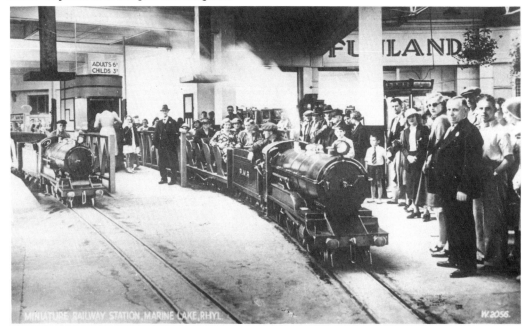

72

TRAMWAYS

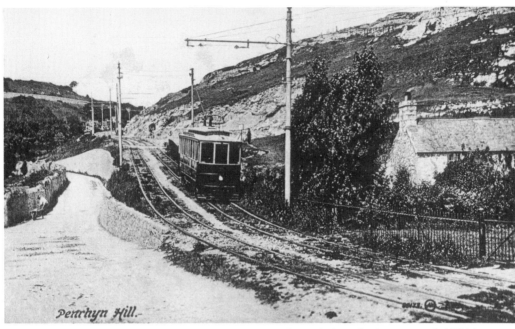

Penrhyn Hill.

73

The Llandudno area was the home of two lines that differed greatly from the 'mainstream' of Welsh narrow gauge lines. The Llandudno and Colwyn Bay Electric Railway which ran on 3ft 6in gauge tracks between those towns had similar counterparts in the Isle of Man and at Burton on Trent, using conventional trams on a light railway running partly through the streets and partly on its own right of way. It was the subject of many commercial cards, (73), published by E. Williams, Penrynside, is typical, showing a tram on the picturesque descent of Penrhyn Hill. Sadly, traffic was steadily lost to the bus and private car and the line closed in 1956.

(74) Llandudno's other line however still thrives. The Great Orme Tramway is also of 3ft 6in gauge, and runs up the Great Orme headland to a height of 637ft o.d. Total length is 1.1 miles with a steepest grade of 1 in 3.6. The line is actually in two distinct sections, and cars are hauled up by a cable running in a centre duct between the rails, the trolley pole merely acting as a pick up for telephone communication between each car and the winding house. Two cars are pictured crossing on the lower section on this 1930's card from Harvey Barton & Sons.

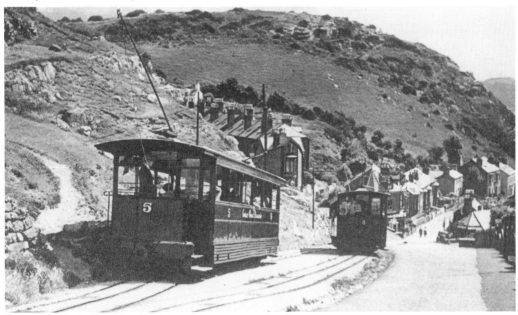

40299   Great Orme Railway, Llandudno

74

41

PENRHYN RAILWAY AND QUARRIES

75

As briefly mentioned in the Introduction, the Welsh narrow gauge railway began with the opening of a two foot (between rail centres) gauge railway from Lord Penrhyn's slate quarries at Bethesda to Port Penrhyn outside Bangor in 1801. This was replaced in October 1879 with a new railway of the same gauge but different route, designed for steam locomotive haulage. As the original DeWinton locomotives soon proved inadequate the Hunslet Engine Co. delivered CHARLES, a powerful 0-4-0ST with 9½in × 12in cylinders, in May 1882. Two sister locos, BLANCHE and LINDA, followed in 1893, and the De Wintons were relegated to quarry duties. Apart from moving slate from quarry to port a passenger service was also provided for the workforce, using simple four wheel roofless carriages. For his monthly visit to view his property however, Lord Penrhyn demanded something more luxurious, so this very plush 14-seat saloon was built. The view (75) of it posed with CHARLES was originally published in the *Locomotive Magazine* for 15 May 1917 and later as a LPC postcard. (76) By the 1950's rail traffic was declining and BLANCHE has only a comparatively short train of empties as her crew prepare to leave Port Penrhyn on 17 August 1957.

76

Kathleen, A Penrhyn Quarry Engine built 1877. Bethesda

BDA.34F

(77) Most North Wales quarry railways had at least one DeWinton vertical boiler loco among their fleet. Built locally at Caernarvon these simple but tough locomotives were usually the first replacement for horse or manual traction. Penrhyn originally had seven plus three horizontal boilered DeWintons for the main line, with the final 1877 pair of vertical boilered ones long outlasting the rest. GEORGE HENRY was retired in 1941 and then kept semi-preserved in the small 'Baldwin' loco shed until presented to the new Narrow Gauge Railway Museum at Towyn in May 1956. Seen here posed for Frith's photographer about 1952 it has had its sister KATHLEEN's name chalked on – perhaps by a mischievous visiting enthusiast? – though the correct nameplate is carried at Towyn.   (78) Frith's cameraman also photographed the engines in the main shed at Coed-y-Parc. On the right is the handsome Manning Wardle 0-4-0ST JUBILEE 1897 with a 'main line' engine and one of the Avonside 0-4-0T's behind, while in the left row is a 'Port' class Hunslet 0-4-0ST and another 'main line' Hunslet 0-4-0ST behind. By this time steam locos were starting to be withdrawn as their boilers or fireboxes became worn beyond economic repair.

BDA 41F.

Penrhyn Quarry , Bethesda

(79) The characteristic cabless 0-4-0ST built by Hunselt for quarry use at Penrhyn were actually of three distinct types, NESTA, built in 1899, being of the 'small quarry' class with 7in × 10in cylinders and a 3ft 3in wheelbase, dimensions shared with the numerically larger 'Alice' class at Dinorwic. She is seen on a 'Maid Marian Locomotive Fund' card resting outside the shed on the Ponc William Parry gallery at the very top of the quarry about 1960. Note her 'tender', a slate rubbish wagon, which was always attached as a handy receptacle for the chains, crowbars, tools, timber packing, etc. for coping with the daily wagon derailments. (80) Rather than buy new, Penrhyn made a number of secondhand purchases of steam locomotives between the Wars. Amongst the best were the four near new Barclay and Avonside locos picked up cheap from Durham County Water Board in 1936 and 1938. CEGIN was one of a pair of Barclay's standard 'E' class 0-4-0WT and remained in use right up to the end of 1964. Always immaculately kept she was photographed basking in the sun on Ponc Ffrith gallery on 4 June 1963, the card issued by IRS in their 'Ken Cooper' series.

PADARN RAILWAY

(81) To move slate to Port Dinorwic where transhipment took place to both ships and the L.N.W.R., Dinorwic quarry's original primitive narrow gauge line was replaced by a conventional railway on a new course, known as the Padarn Railway, and built to the unusual gauge of 4ft 0in. The slate wagons (of Dinorwic's own distinctive wooden design) were run on to transporter wagons and taken seven miles to Pen-Scoins where they were run off and lowered down a narrow gauge incline to the Port. A rake of loaded wagons, complete with miniscule brake van, is seen in the tranship sidings at Gilfach-ddu, a most unusual subject for a 'commercial' postcard: the publisher in this case being Jerome Ltd. (82) After five years of horse working, two peculiar 0-4-0's by Alfred Horlock and Co. of Northfleet were introduced on to the Padarn Railway, being in turn replaced from 1882 onwards by three more conventional Hunslet 0-6-0T's which remained in use until closure of the railway on 27 October 1961. DINORWIC (HE302/1881) the oldest of the three awaits the right-away at Gilfach-ddu with a loaded train in 1957. Unlike the near total preservation of their narrow gauge sisters, all three were scrapped in 1963 after half-hearted efforts to preserve one.

DINORWIC QUARRIES

83

(83) As at Penrhyn, the principal motive power at Dinorwic slate quarries were little cabless Hunslet 0-4-0ST's, designated the 'Alice' class, the original name of KING OF THE SCARLETS, seen at work high up in the quarry in 1957. Dimensionally they were very similar to Penrhyn's 'small quarry' class (see (79)) but there were various differences such as the sloping frame ends and side dumb buffers. Unlike Penrhyn, where steam haulage was latterly confined to shunting on the waste tips, Dinorwic used steam throughout the quarry almost to the end. (84) In contrast to Penrhyn, Dinorwic purchased only three secondhand steam locomotives, including an Avonside and a Barclay in 1949 and 1948 respectively. These two were originally part of the large fleet employed to build Burnhope reservoir in Weardale, Co. Durham from where Penrhyn had bought five locos pre-War. Dinorwic's Avonside 0-4-0T was christened ELIDIR but the Barclay simply retained its original running number, 70. ELIDIR, seen shunting at Gilfach-ddu about 1952, was exported to Toronto in July 1966, and her name is perpetuated on an ex Dinorwic 0-4-0ST (formerly RED DAMSEL) now running on the Llanberis Lake Railway.

84

(85) For working the ¾ mile long Peris Tramway between the slate mills at Hafod Owen and the Padarn Railway exchange sidings at Gilfach-ddu something more powerful than the cabless quarry locomotives was needed. Accordingly Hunslet built two handsome 'Mills Class' 0-4-0ST with 8½in × 14in cylinders, a domed boiler, central buffers and an ingenious treadle on the footplate which uncoupled the train when pressed. Originally named VAENOL (Hunslet 638 of 1895) and PORT DINORWIC (HE671/1898) they were later renamed JERRY M and CACKLER. On this anonymous photographic card JERRY M is seen resting outside the locomotive shops at Gilfach-ddu (still used today by the Llanberis Lake Railway) in May 1935. (86) In early 1906 the Hunslet monopoly in supplying locomotives to Dinorwic was broken when their latest quote was rejected by Dinorwic's Manager, Ernest Neal, and a cheaper offer from W. G. Bagnall accepted instead. Although remaining a 'one off' at Llanberis SYBIL (Bagnall 1760 of 1906), a cabless version of the standard 7in × 12in cylindered design, gave good service at Dinorwic, even if the marine boiler did require more careful firing than the conventional Hunslet one. SYBIL remained in use until about 1962 and is now preserved in Cornwall. This is another excellent 'real photographic' card published by the Maid Marian Locomotive Fund.

The original pair of Hunslet saddletanks built for shunting the narrow gauge tracks at Port Dinorwic were transferred to the quarry and replaced by two new Hunslet locomotives of a slightly different design in 1922. Like their predecessors, No. 1 (originally LADY JOAN) and DOLBADARN had full length deep pitched frames but the boiler pressure was increased to 160psi, full cabs fitted and safety valve and whistle mounted on the flat dome. DOLBADARN moved up to the quarry in 1935 but No. 1 remained at the Port until closure of the Padarn Railway in 1961 made her redundant. Latterly she was assisted by a Ruston diesel and No. 70, the 'E' class Barclay 0-4-0WT purchased secondhand from Durham in 1938. Our two photographic cards show (87) No. 1 as originally built hard at work at Port Dinorwic in 1947 and (88) (a 'Maid Marian Fund' card) depicts her shunting near the slate mills at Hafod Owen in her latter days (1966). Note that for quarry use the cab has been removed, chimney shortened and central sprung buffers replaced with side dumb blocks. She was sold for preservation in 1967 and currently resides in preservation in Hampshire, with her cab replaced.

88

48

89

(89) The Welsh quarries included a wonderful variety of types within the locomotive fleets but MOLE (later renamed ALGERNON) was surely amongst the strangest. The builder was J. H. Wilson & Co., Ltd. of Liverpool, whose main product was steam cranes, although patents for ships steering gear, winches, excavator buckets and portable water closets were also held: parts of all these, plus a return-flue launch type boiler, appear to have been utilised in MOLE's construction. At any rate, her new owners seem to have been very proud of her. The quarry manager and driver pose with their new charge after taking delivery on the Welsh Slate Co. quay at Portmadoc about 1880.   (90) Apart from their work for the Festiniog, N.W.N.G.R. and Talyllyn Railways, the Spooner family acted as consulting engineers on a wide variety of local railway and quarry matters. KATHLEEN was designed by G. P. Spooner and built by Vulcan Foundry (their No. 805 of 1877) for the Alexandra Slate Quarry at Moel Tryfan in which the Spooner family had an interest. Two similar locos were built for the neighbouring Braich Quarry and the family likeness with the F.R. and N.W.N.G.R. Vulcan Foundry locos is readily apparent.

90

91

These two 'enthusiast' photographic cards depict examples of Bagnall saddle tanks cut down by their owners to suit restricted clearances. (91) WENDY (Bagnall 2091 of 1919) was a standard 6in × 9in cylinder design delivered to the Votty and Bowydd slate quarries at Blaenau Festiniog, but saw little use there. In March 1930 she was sold to the Dorothea Quarry at Nantlle who cut down chimney and awning and enclosed the latter. Seen here at work in 1934 it had been withdrawn by 1940 and lay derelict outside the slate mill until rescued for preservation in 1961 by the Hampshire Narrow Gauge Railway Society who have painstakingly restored her to original condition. (92) POWERFUL (Bagnall 1901 of 1911) was of the larger 7in × 12in cylindered type and spent all its life at the 2ft 10½in gauge system at Kneeshaw Lupton & Co. Ltd.'s quarries at Llysfaen, near Llandulas, Denbighshire. Some time after 1935 its chimney and cab were cut down as seen here. It was replaced in 1948 by a new 48DL class Ruston diesel (also with a 'one off' cab) and then lay derelict in the quarry until cut up in 1958.

92

(93) Three little maids . . . Hunslet 0-4-0ST's UNA and SYBIL line up with the 1877 DeWinton CHALONER outside their shed on the top level at Pen-yr-Orsedd quarry, one sunny day about 1950. This quarry formed the eastern terminus of the Nantlle Tramroad and like several other quarries served by that line it had a considerable amount of mixed 2ft and 3ft 6in gauge track around its slate mills. Note the 'blondins' (aerial ropeways) in the background, used to lower slate wagons down on to the quarry floor way below. Happily all three locomotives shown here were saved and, beautifully restored, can be seen in occasional use at Llanberis, Brecon Mountain and Leighton Buzzard respectively.   (94) When the G.W.R. took over and converted to standard gauge the little Festiniog and Blaenau Railway they inherited the slate traffic from the quarries at Manod, above Blaenau Festiniog. For slate that was routed via the Festiniog Railway the G.W.R. built their own slate wagons for the quarries to use, and moved them on these 'piggy back' flat wagons to a tranship dock in the G.W.R. yard at Blaenau. This Photomatic card shows what may be a G.W.R. 'official' view of two of their staff posed with such a wagon at Blaenau, probably around 1920.

95

(95) The four large slate quarries around Blaenau Festiniog were all pioneers in the use of alternatives to steam locomotive traction for surface work and, more importantly, to replace animal or manual haulage underground. Llechwedd Slate Quarries installed their own power station as early as 1904, then in 1926-7 electrified part of their rail system with D.C. overhead wiring. To work it they bought a small B.E.V. loco and converted two of their three Bagnall steam locos to electric traction using the original frames, wheels, coupling rods and cab, bought in motors and new bodywork. Topically named THE COALITION and THE ECLIPSE, the former is seen on the main No. 5 level about 1970.   (96) Llechwedd's neighbour Maenofferen quarries primarily favoured diesel locomotives, buying one of the earliest Motor Rail diesels in 1929. However like most slate quarries it preferred Ruston and Hornsby locos, whose transmission design allowed the driver to walk alongside and act as his own shunter. Certain Rustons were fitted with exhaust washers for underground use but this 1935 18/21hp machine was still virtually as built when it was photographed in July 1978 outside the slate mill. Note the typical double flanged wagon wheels and stub points.

96

(97) The Penmaenmawr granite quarries had an **extensive fleet** of steam and internal combustion locomotives including a number of DeWinton vertical boilered locomotives. As the quarry system was of 3ft gauge they differed from their slate quarry counterparts in having inside frames. Amongst the last to remain in service was WATKIN which became a familiar sight to so many a holidaymaker and traveller on the adjoining Holyhead-Chester line in the 1950's and 1960's. Originally used for shunting under the stone hoppers by the main line sidings, its final duty was as a stationary boiler and then lay derelict until preserved. This undated view is from another excellent Photomatic card.   (98) Gold has been mined intermittently in the Dolgellau area from Roman times up to the present day. Virtually all the mines had underground 'tramroads' constructed initially with wooden or iron rails. From the 1880's onwards local photographers took posed views at such mines and would include as many miners and 'gaffers' as possible to maximise sales of the resultant photo! This c.1900 example includes a good view of a typical 'tramway' – note the crude bridge rail track and the small mine tub, small enough to be manhandled below ground.

99

Industrial narrow gauge railways in North Wales are traditionally associated with the slate and stone quarries of Caernarvon and Merioneth but our last two illustrations show examples from industries situated further east.

(99) The Castle Firebrick Co. Ltd. ran a fleet of Kerr, Stuart 'Wren' and 6in Bagnall 0-4-0ST's on the two foot gauge tramway linking the claypits with their brickworks near Mold. Superseded by road transport in 1948, one 'Wren' and two Bagnalls were retained in the hope of finding a good home for them. Despite the modest asking price of £5(!) each, no-one was interested and after 10 years they were cut up, a far cry from the inflated prices being asked for such machines today. On a photographic card from the IRS H. W. Robinson collection, 'new type Wren' No. 1 (KS4005/18) is seen at work about 1932.   (100) On this the final illustration your author seeks the reader's indulgence to stray just over the border into England . . . at Porth-y-Waen Limeworks near Oswestry the quarries had a pair of 7in Bagnall saddletanks on the quarry rail system. Built to the unusual gauge of 4ft 0in, they were constructed as late as 1931 (No. 1, WB2466) and 1933 (No. 2, WB2497) but nevertheless were cut up on site after rail traffic ceased in May 1951.

100

ABOUT PLATEWAY PRESS

Plateway Press was formed in 1986 by Andrew Neale and Keith Taylorson, with the aim of producing good quality books on neglected aspects of the railway and transport scene, without arbitrary restrictions on cover prices. The imprint was originally based in Church Road, Croydon, on the course of the erstwhile Surrey Iron Railway, an early 'Plateway' providing the inspiration for our name. Since 1988 the operation has been run from Brighton. Our catalogue of titles currently in print will be sent on request: a selection of those available is described below.

BAGNALL NARROW GAUGE LOCOMOTIVES AND ROLLING STOCK 1910 (Edited) Andrew Neale

Abridged facsimile reprint of a locomotive and rolling stock catalogue published by W. G. Bagnall Ltd., Castle Engine Works, Stafford. Issued just before World War 1 it illustrates and describes a selection of locos built by Bagnalls between 1893 and 1910. All are narrow gauge and range from tiny 1' 7'' gauge 0-4-0T to 3' 0'' gauge 4-6-0T, but with the smaller 'industrial' type locomotives predominating. Virtually all were exported to customers in countries as far apart as Uruguay, Japan, Egypt, Chile, Burma, India, Formosa, South Africa and Mexico. The illustrated pages are exact facsimiles of those in the original catalogue, a separate Appendix gives further details of the locomotives illustrated (gauge, dimensions, known customers, etc.), and the introduction is written by leading Bagnall expert Allan C. Baker. Also included are facsimiles of pages illustrating a representative selection of rolling stock and trackwork.

64 pages, illustrated throughout, ISBN 1 871980 09 X   **Price £6.95**

THE CALSHOT AND FAWLEY NARROW GAUGE RAILWAYS by F. W. Cooper

Completely updated history of a fascinating group of 2' 0'' gauge railways in Hampshire. The RAF Calshot Railway was originally a contractor's line, used in the construction of the RAF station, and was later expanded to provide a transport service for the base, conveying materials and servicemen, until closure in 1945. Locomotives included Robert Hudson 0-4-0WT, Kerr Stuart 'Wren' and Barclay 0-4-0WT, one of which survives as the Talyllyn Railway's DOUGLAS. Plus story of the railway serving the Anglo-Gulf West Indies refinery from 1920-1961: this provided a complete integrated transport system for this large oil refinery at Fawley, Hants, conveying men and materials, and boasted a fire-fighting train! Motive power steam and petrol including ex World War 1 'Simplex' types.

Illustrated throughout with many interesting and historically valuable photos of both systems. Includes track diagrams, locomotive and wagon drawings.

64 pages, 42 black and white photos, 10 maps and drawings, ISBN 0 9511108 7 X   **Price 6.50**

THE GROUDLE GLEN RAILWAY by David H. Smith

Revised and updated history of the 2' 0'' gauge railway near Douglas, Isle of Man. Opened in 1896, this was the first purpose built public 'pleasure' railway in Britain, and conveyed visitors to a small zoo, whose inhabitants provided inspiration for the names of the line's two Bagnall 2-4-0T's SEA LION and POLAR BEAR. The railway closed in 1962 but in the 1980's was substantially recreated on its original site by volunteers. This book contains a full history of the 'old' railway and the first ever detailed account of the railway's restoration. Details are provided of the two steam locos (both of which survive), and of other motive power, coaches, train operation, fares, tickets, etc. There are scale drawings of both steam locomotives, battery electric loco, and two types of coach.

56 pages, 2 colour and 30 black & white illustrations, 7 maps and drawings, ISBN 1 871980 00 3 **Price £5.75**

SELECT BIBLIOGRAPHY

There have been innumerable books dealing with Welsh narrow gauge railways published over the years: the following have been selected as not only being good books on their subject, but also currently (1991) in print.

NARROW GAUGE RAILWAYS IN MID WALES   J. I. C. Boyd   (Oakwood Press)
— covers Corris, Talyllyn, Fairbourne, Rheidol, Glyn Valley, Welshpool and Llanfair and minor industrial lines in mid Wales.

NARROW GAUGE RAILWAYS OF NORTH CAERNARVONSHIRE   J. I. C. Boyd   (Oakwood Press)
  VOLUME 1 — Nantlle Tramroad, Snowdon Mountain Railway, Pwlheli horse tramways, minor quarry railways.
  VOLUME 2 — Penrhyn Quarry Railways.
  VOLUME 3 — Dinorwic Quarry Railway, Great Orme Tramway, Penmaenmawr Granite Railway, Conway Valley n.g. industrial railways.

NARROW GAUGE RAILWAYS OF SOUTH CAERNARVONSHIRE   J. I. C. Boyd   (Oakwood Press)
  VOLUME 1 — Gorseddau, Croesor and Portmadoc Embankment tramways, Festiniog and Blaenau Rly, N.W.N.G.R. and P.B.S.S.R.
  VOLUME 2 — Welsh Highland Railway.

THE TALYLLYN RAILWAY   J. I. C. Boyd   (Wild Swan Publications)
— comprehensive history up to 1951.

THE CORRIS RAILWAY   L. Cozens   (Corris Railway Society)

RETURN TO CORRIS   Corris Railway Society   (Avon-Anglia)

THE VALE OF RHEIDOL RAILWAY   C. C. Green   (Wild Swan Publications)

THE GLYN VALLEY TRAMWAY   W. J. Milner   (OPC)

THE TALYLLYN RAILWAY   D. Potter   (David & Charles)
— thorough coverage of the Railway in the 'Preservation' era.

THE WELSHPOOL AND LLANFAIR RAILWAY   R. T. Russell and R. I. Cartwright   (David & Charles)

VERTICAL BOILER LOCOMOTIVES   R. A. S. Abbott   (Oakwood Press)
— includes a section on DeWinton locomotives.

THE FESTINIOG RAILWAY (Vols. 1 and 2)   J. I. C. Boyd   (Oakwood Press)
— comprehensive history of the F.R. from inception through to the 'Preservation' era.*

SLATE FROM BLAENAU   J. G. Isherwood   (A.B. Publishing)

TALIESIN-FESTINIOG RAILWAY LOCOMOTIVES   (A.B. Publishing)

* Currently out of print but copies of various editions easily available.
  Likely to be reprinted during the life of this volume.